FEMALE SPORTS STARS

Superstars of Women's Basketball

Superstars of Women's Figure Skating

Superstars of Women's Golf

Superstars of Women's Gymnastics

Superstars of Women's Tennis

Superstars of Women's Track and Field

CHELSEA HOUSE PUBLISHERS

SUPERSTARS OF WOMEN'S GOLF

Barry Wilner

CHELSEA HOUSE PUBLISHERS
Philadelphia

CHELSEA HOUSE PUBLISHERS

Produced by Daniel Bial Agency and Associates
New York, New York

Senior Designer   Cambraia Magalhães
Picture Research   Sandy Jones
Cover Illustration   Bill Vann
Frontispiece photo   Nancy Lopez

First Printing
1   3   5   7   9   8   6   4   2

Library of Congress Cataloguing-in-Publication Data

Wilner, Barry
        Superstars of women's golf / Barry Wilner
            p.   cm. — (Female sports stars)
        Includes bibiliographical references (p.) and index.
        ISBN 0-7910-4390-8 (Hard)
        1. Women golfers—Biography—Juvenile literature. 2. Women
golfers—History—Juvenile literature. [1. Golfers. 2. Women—
Biography.] I. Title. II. Series.
GV964.A1W55   1997
796.352'092'2—dc20
[B]   96-45754
                                                                        CIP
                                                                        A C

CONTENTS

WOMENS OPEN
AT HOLE
30
PLAYER
UNDER
AT HO
RAWLS
5
54
BERG
3
ZAHARIAS
3
SUGGS
E
ADIES
76

1

EARLY DAYS

You can go all the way back to the last century to find inspiring and entertaining stories about professional golf—men's professional golf.

From the early days of the British Open through the turn of the century and all the way to the 1940s, men dominated the sport when it was played for pay.

Not until 1948, when the Women's Professional Golf Association was formed, did women get much attention on the course. Except for the legendary Babe Didrikson Zaharias, probably the best female athlete ever, and the great Patty Berg, stardom eluded the early pioneers of the game.

The WPGA did not last and was replaced by the LPGA in 1950. "It was important for us to organize a women's tour," Berg said. "We

Four great golfers dominated the leaderboards in the 1950s—from left to right, Betsy Rawls, Patty Berg, Louise Suggs, and Babe Didrikson Zaharias.

felt we needed a chance to show what we could do, just as the men could show their stuff on their tour."

Berg, Zaharias, Fred Corcoran—who had run the men's tour and was an excellent promoter—and the president of the Wilson Sporting Goods Company, I. C. Icely, met in Miami to start up the LPGA. "Louise Suggs, the Babe, me, Marlene and Alice Bauer, Betty Dodd, Peggy Kirk Bell and Betsy Rawls. I guess we made up the corps of the first LPGA tournaments," Berg said. "There wasn't a lot of money or a lot of attention, but we were determined.

"We were followed in time by Mickey Wright, Kathy Whitworth and so many others. Lo and behold, from that Miami meeting and the seed we planted has sprung the great LPGA of today, the great women's golf explosion of today."

Berg was one of the early legends, and a true leader. Like Babe Didrikson Zaharias, she was a terrific all-around athlete. She grew up in Minneapolis, Minnesota, just seven doors down from Charles "Bud" Wilkinson. Wilkinson became a stand-out college quarterback; as coach of the Oklahoma University Sooners, his team set a record by winning 47 consecutive games.

Baseball, football, hockey—Berg, Wilkinson, and the local kids played them all together. Berg often played quarterback, but after she lost several teeth in rough play, Wilkinson convinced her to give it up.

Berg then took up competitive speed ice skating and won several medals. She took up golf and entered the Minneapolis City championship. She came in last, putting so many balls in the water she needed to borrow balls from her opponent. But she devoted the next

JoAnne "Big Mama" Carner exults after blasting a shot out of deep water.

year to practice and came back to win the tournament the next year—at age 15.

Berg won 57 tournaments and has been named to six Halls of Fame. She was also the first president of the LPGA.

In fact, Berg believes the surge in golf's popularity stems from reaching out to children. "I think one of the things that boomed golf was the junior programs," said Berg, a three-time winner of the *Associated Press* Woman Athlete of the Year award. "Then the introduction to high school and college for both men and women and then there is the teaching, television, merchandising, virtually no limits on women's play at country clubs and the simple fact that you can play at any age, like me."

Kathy Whitworth has more career victories to her name—88—than any other pro player.

The final measure of greatness for women's golfers is qualifying for the LPGA Hall of Fame. It is the hardest hall to make because it is based only on performance. No popularity contests or votes.

To make the Hall of Fame, a woman must belong to the LPGA for 10 straight years and have won at least 30 events, including two major tournaments (the U.S. Women's Open, the LPGA Championship, the Dinah Shore or the du Maurier Canadian Classic), or 35 tournaments with at least one major, or 40 tourneys with no majors.

Patty Berg was one of the first inductees, having taken 57 pro career victories and 85 altogether, including 15 majors. "Her contribution to the LPGA is without equal," said Charles Mechem, a former commissioner of the tour. "But I think to limit one's comments about Patty to the LPGA is far too narrow."

Indeed, Berg—who became a champion one year after her first round as an amateur, when she shot a 122—has her name on a cancer wing of a hospital in her hometown of Fort Myers, Florida. She is as tireless in her work for charity as she was on the course.

Berg and Zaharias were the biggest stars of the LPGA's early days. Together, they brought enough interest to the tour that it tripled in size to 21 events in 1952.

The golfers often traveled together in groups. There was little prize money available in those years, when even the men didn't play for huge purses, so many of the players would drive from city to city. "Sometimes, we'd drive all night to the next tournament and almost get out of the car and tee it up," said Louise Suggs, another top player of that era who won exactly 50 times, including an amazing eight victories in 19 appearances in 1953. "It was an exciting time.

"One day, I started figuring what 50 tournaments wins would be worth at today's prices and had to stop, because I got sick. But the foundation had to be built and most of today's players appreciate what was accomplished in the beginning."

Suggs was one of the Big Four, along with Berg, Babe, and Betty Jameson. They were the founders of the tour and the first inductees into the Hall of Fame.

They also had sponsors to back them on tour; sponsors gave the players money to use their products. Berg played for Wilson and Suggs for McGregor, two of the biggest makers of golf equipment. "You have to give a lot of credit to the players who didn't have sponsors," Suggs said. "They hung on, with everybody trying to support everybody else, and helped make the tour what it is today."

Today, the LPGA is one of the great success stories of sports, with more than $25 million in prize money and 38 tour events, 26 of which are televised. Every player on the current tour knows she owes a debt to the pioneers. "Without their strength and their sacrifices to make women's golf work, where would we be?" said Nancy Lopez, the greatest women's player of the modern era.

Lopez referred not only to Zaharias, Berg, Suggs and Jameson, but to the next wave of champions: Betsy Rawls, Mickey Wright, Marlene Hagge and Kathy Whitworth. And to the 1970s group that helped the tour prosper just before Lopez arrived: Sandra Haynie, Carol Mann and Joanne Carner.

Wright was considered to have the perfect swing, and she used it to win 82 pro events. She won the U.S. Women's Open and the LPGA Championship four times apiece and from 1959-68, she won an average of eight times a season. "The women who came before me, with their beautiful golf swings —Louise Suggs and Petty Berg — they were a big influence on me," Wright said. "The people who played golf, both profes-

Mickey Wright won 82 pro events and was considered to have the perfect swing.

sionally and as amateurs, in that era played for the love of it. I suppose it was because there were so few tournaments, so few women golfers, that the game was really the thing. That sort of set the tone for my whole life."

One of Wright's practice exercises was to play nine holes with one club, and she even shot par for the nine holes several times, using a 6 iron.

Wright always insisted that to do well on the course, you had to simply enjoy the round and not think about numbers. Obviously, that way worked well for her. "The worst mistakes golfers can make are to get down on themselves during a round, or think about scoring," she said. "If you want to guarantee you won't score well, just think about scoring.

"If you feel like you have to make a birdie, then your attention is not on hitting the ball down the middle of the fairway, hitting it on the green and letting come-what-may happen. There aren't many people good enough to make things happen."

Wright was one person good enough. But she quit golf in 1980 after undergoing an operation on her lip for a form of skin cancer. "It was from being out in the sun for so many years," she said. She also had foot surgery twice for nerve problems.

In 1985, Wright and Whitworth teamed to play in the Legends of Golf event against a field of stars from the men's Senior Tour. It was an honor long deserved. "I think it's great," said Bob Toski, considered the top teaching pro in golf at the time. "It's nice to see anyone who has the ability to play here. And they definitely deserve to be in the tournament. They are great athletes. They are Legends, indeed."

Whitworth holds the record for official career victories with 88, more than any man or woman. Seven times, she was Player of the Year. Whitworth won six majors, including three LPGA Championships, and already was in the Hall of Fame 15 years before she actually retired from the tour.

Always a favorite among fans and fellow players, Whitworth gave back to her sport by serving three terms as LPGA president. "I wasn't out to prove anything or do it for a noble cause," said Whitworth, who along with Zaharias and Wright was nominated for Golfer of the Century in 1988, an award won by Jack Nicklaus. "I enjoyed the life, the girls, the traveling and the competition. I just committed myself to getting better every time I went out and played. If I did that, I always believed everything else would take care of itself."

In 1962, Whitworth won her first pro tournament in Baltimore. It was her third year on the LPGA tour and she collected $1,000 for the victory. Players pay their caddies more than that each week nowadays.

Soon, she was dominating women's golf, and after Whitworth stopped playing, she became one of the game's best teachers. "If not for people like Kathy, we wouldn't have the opportunity to play out here," said current LPGA player Tammie Green. "She's such a great role model for so many people, and she goes out of her way to do things for the game."

Whitworth had a terrific rivalry with Carner, who won 23 tournaments in the 1970s. It was "The Whit vs. Big Mama" when they met. "I chased her for years and never really did catch her," Carner said. "Everyone likes her, because she always treated people with such respect and worked so hard to improve the LPGA."

Carner was a ground breaker, too. A native of the Seattle area, she was the first woman at Arizona State University to receive an athletic scholarship in any sport. "A friend of mine used to work for the racetrack in the Phoenix area and played golf with the president of the university," Carner said. "He asked whether I ever thought about going out of state. He wrote and told them that I practiced with the rain running off my hair, and living in Arizona, the people there thought it was fabulous."

Carner got into golf because of her siblings. She used to hunt for lost golf balls with her brother at a nine-hole public course about four miles from her home. They would look for balls all week and sell them on the weekend. "Then we'd take all the neighborhood kids to the movies," she recalled. "We'd make maybe $20 to $40 on a Saturday selling them."

Joanne's brother Bill worked at night watering the golf course and her two sisters worked in the snack bar at another course. "They had a rule that anybody who worked there had to learn to play," she said. "They started playing and the course had these rental clubs with hickory shafts that would either split or warp. They would throw them out in a barrel and we would ask to take them and my dad would fix them up and we would hit balls in the pasture."

Carner credits the help of her husband, Don, for her success in golf. She met him after she left college, at a Miami golf tournament he entered as an amateur. He would attend every lesson Joanne took from various touring and teaching pros. "After a while, he got almost better than the teachers and so knowledgeable about my swing," she said. "And he is the only one to help me with my putting."

In 1976, just before Lopez would take the tour by storm and lift it to another popularity level, Carner got her nickname. She and Sandra Palmer were tied in the 1976 U.S. Women's Open after 72 holes. They went to an 18-hole playoff the next day, and Palmer said, "I am going against Big Mama."

"The caddies loved it and picked it up and it has stuck with me ever since," Carner said. "When I get thin, they shorten it to Mama."

Big Mama entered the Hall of Fame in 1982 and, until recently, still made appearances on the tour. The rest of the trail blazers of women's golf play rarely. But their contributions never will be forgotten.

2

BABE DIDRIKSON ZAHARIAS

Choosing an athlete as the greatest in his or her sport is a very difficult job. Is Michael Jordan the best basketball player ever? Was Jim Brown the number one football player? It's impossible to get everyone to agree.

Yet when sports fans discuss who is the greatest woman athlete ever, one name always is mentioned: Mildred Ella Didrikson Zaharias, best known as Babe.

For Babe, the game didn't matter. She was an Olympic champion, a basketball standout, and the first star of women's golf. Babe could beat most men at tennis, handball, and bowling. She was a fine baseball player. Even in male-oriented sports such as football, boxing, and lacrosse, she was willing to give it a try. Usually, she excelled.

Once, in an exhibition, she struck out Joe DiMaggio. She won a team title in the national

Babe Didrikson Zaharias almost singlehandedly created the pro women's golf tour.

track and field championships by herself, competing in eight events and winning five—the 80-meter hurdles, shot put, long jump, javelin, and baseball throw. She led an amateur basketball team to three straight national titles.

"I've always been taught that if you are going to compete, you should do it as well as you possibly can," Babe said. "That means being in the best shape you can be and being ready to do everything you can to win."

In 1932, a 19-year-old Babe won gold medals in the javelin and the 80-meter hurdles at the Olympic Games held that year in Los Angeles. The rules of the time limited her to three events. She was disqualified in the high jump because she dived over the bar head-first, which was then considered illegal.

That same year, Babe won *The Associated Press* Woman Athlete of the Year award for the first of five times. She also got it in 1945, 1946, 1947 and 1950—as a golfer.

Born in Port Arthur, Texas, the daughter of a Norwegian carpenter who insisted his children be physically fit, Babe never picked up a golf club during her formative years.

At age 18, Babe was in Dallas shopping for a dress when she noticed a golf set in a green-trimmed bag in the window of a sporting goods store. She bought the clubs, even though she never had played golf.

Off she went to a public course in Dallas, and she practiced swinging the club. At first, she admitted, it was "odd." She was more used to the way you swing a baseball bat. But her natural skills took over. She got the basics of a golf swing down and decided to play a round.

Normally, a first-time golfer is lucky to keep the score in the 110-120 range. Babe shot a 95,

which could have been much lower if she understood how to read putting greens and hit out of sand traps.

"I could hit the ball a long way right from the start," she said. "I could hit it as far as the men, and I could be pretty accurate. But I had to learn so much about the short game [shots from close to the green and putting]."

The next step was golf lessons. Babe went to the Dallas Country Club and club pro Pat Green taught her the ins and outs of the sport. As usual, she was a quick learner and, after three sessions with Green, Babe shot an 83.

Her golf career would have to wait, though. In 1932, Babe headed for Los Angeles and

One of the greatest athletes ever, Zaharias also was a pretty good harmonica player. Here even as she's making a recording with Betsy Dodd (left), she had her golf clubs near by.

became an international star with her gold-medal performances.

Such stardom led a promoter to pay her $3,500 a week—a fortune in the 1930s—to go on tour as a singer and harmonica player. Of course, Babe was good at those things, too.

But she hated it and, one week into the tour, she quit. "I want to be doing things outdoors and in sports," she said. "I need to see the sky. I need to be out in the fresh air."

Where better to be there, do that, than on the golf course? The great sports writer Grantland Rice convinced Babe to take up golf seriously. "I told her she could be the greatest golfer in the world if she spent time at the game," Rice said. "Babe could do anything well if she was interested, and golf was a great challenge for her."

More than a year after her lessons with Green, Babe broke 100 on the tough Brentwood (California) Country Club. She did it with borrowed golf shoes and clubs.

Babe shooting out of a trap in the 1946 National Women's Amateur Golf championship—which she won.

She also needed enough money to be able to quit her job at a Dallas insurance company, Employers Casualty, and play golf full-time. So Babe played baseball and basketball on tour, often facing major leaguers and former college stars. When she returned to her job, Employers Casualty paid for her lessons at the Dallas Country Club.

Then things went sour. Babe was seen in magazine and newspaper advertisements for Dodge automobiles, and she was driving a new red Dodge that, on her salary as a secretary, she barely could afford. She explained that Dodge used her name and photograph without her permission and that she was paying off the car with her earnings.

The Amateur Athletic Union, which was in charge of most non-professional sports in the United States at the time—but not golf—didn't believe her. When Babe gave the AAU letters from the Dodge dealer that proved what she claimed, the AAU offered to reinstate her as an amateur. Instead, she hired a manager and began getting paid for athletic appearances. It was not until 1937, nearly five full years later, that she regained her amateur status.

In 1934, after months of private lessons and work on her golf game—some days, Babe would hit 1,500 balls, continuing even when her hands began to blister and bleed, "I always had to wear tape on them," she said—she entered the Fort Worth (Texas) Invitational.

Babe won her first match with a 77, a great feat for a first-timer. Even though she lost her second match to an experienced player, it was obvious golf soon would be another sport she would master. "I love the competition," she said. "Not only are you playing against another play-

er, you're playing against the golf course. Every hole is different, a new challenge. Every round, the hole can be different because of the wind or the pin placement [the hole is moved to different areas of the green each day]."

In April 1935, Babe entered the Texas Women's Amateur Open, one of the most important tournaments. And she won. "I was on top of the world," she said. "It had taken me longer than I originally figured it would to get going, but at last I was rolling in golf."

That roll didn't last long in amateur golf. Several players complained to the U.S. Golf Association that Babe was a pro in other sports and should not be allowed in amateur events. The USGA agreed and banned Babe.

So she toured the country doing exhibitions with men golfers, including future Hall of Famer Gene Sarazen, a star on the men's tour. She attracted huge crowds and sponsors fought to have her appear on their behalf.

"It's a sort of lonely business, being a woman pro," she said. "There's no Women's Open or pro championships to play in."

In 1938, Babe moved to California, where she could play all year. She entered the Los Angeles Open, which had no rules against a women playing with the men. She didn't make the cut, but she met George Zaharias, a famous professional wrestler. They began dating, even though their schedules meant they didn't see each other too often. In December 1938, they were married. They went on a six-month honeymoon in Australia, where she gave clinics and played exhibitions. George became her manager.

He also urged Babe to reapply for her amateur status. She did, but was told she must

In 1951, Babe Didrikson Zaharias (left) joined Patty Berg and four other Americans at Sunningdale to take on the British pros—both men and women.

wait three years and not make any money playing golf. Babe was willing to do that and, even though she won the only two women's pro events in 1940—the Western Open and Texas Open—she did not collect the prize money.

The USGA reinstated her in January 1944. "I don't think I've ever been happier in my life," she said.

Or better. Babe began winning right away. She even won the 1945 Western Open despite the death of her mother during the tournament. Babe, legend has it, sat in her hotel room for hours, playing the harmonica, to soothe the pain of her mother's death. Then she won the final match.

She won five straight tournaments in 1946, then told George she wanted a break. He urged her to continue playing until her streak ended. Babe did—and the winning streak reached 15!

George talked Babe into entering the 1947 British Ladies Amateur in Scotland. Babe was stunned to find herself just as popular overseas as she was in the States. "The people were so wonderful to me," she said. "They made me feel like one of their own like royalty."

Babe did not bring the proper clothing for the damp, cold weather in Scotland, and when she told several sportswriters, her problem was printed in Scottish newspapers. The next day, dozens of outfits of warm clothes arrived at her hotel. Babe picked out some slacks and a jacket, then gave the rest of the clothes to needy people.

No American had ever won the British Ladies. In the final, Jacqueline Gordon of England led Babe by two holes through 11 in the 36-hole match. But Babe rallied, tying the match halfway through, then winning five of the first six holes in the afternoon. That was enough to win.

Back in the United States, she extended the winning string to 17, then turned pro again in August because she was offered $300,000 for a movie. But she had another reason. "I had reached the pinnacle of amateur golf," she said. "Pro golf was still a challenge. I hoped by turning pro, I would better women's golf by forcing more open tournaments."

In 1949, Babe and George started the Ladies Professional Golf Association. The LPGA began with all of eight members, but Babe's popularity helped it take hold in the United States. Soon, it had 30 players, and it kept right on growing.

In 1950, Babe was selected as the top woman athlete of the half-century by *The Associated Press*, the highest honor given to anyone in female sports. But in 1952, she began to struggle. She tired easily. She won a tournament in Beaumont, Texas, even though she could barely walk. The next day, she was told she had cancer.

Surgery was performed and Babe thought she might never play golf again. Slowly, though, she began to recover and less than four months after her operation, Babe played in the 1953 All-American Tournament, finishing 15th.

Amazingly, she led the World Championship the next week through 3 1/2 rounds before fading to third. Babe was given the Ben Hogan Award for her courageous comeback.

For the next year, she won a few tournaments, including the Women's Open, but she still was tiring easily. When she dramatically won at Spartanburg, South Carolina, for her 82nd career victory, Babe collapsed at the end of the event. Doctors discovered more cancer. They couldn't operate this time.

Babe and George started the Babe Zaharias Cancer Fund. She exercised as much as she could, but she soon became bed-ridden. On September 27, 1956, at the age of 43, the greatest women's athlete of all time died.

Almost single-handedly, Babe Didrikson put women's golf on the map. But she never knew how popular the sport would soon become.

3

NANCY LOPEZ

F rom the time she was seven years old, Nancy Lopez was a golfer. When she was 12, she was beating high school and college players. Before she was 20, she had won all kinds of amateur and college golfing awards.

Stardom as a professional soon followed. Of all the great women golfers of the last two decades, Nancy Lopez has been the biggest star, the most popular, and, for many of those years, the best player.

"It took her about one year, then she made an outstanding impact," wrote Kathy Whitworth, a Hall of Fame golfer who holds the record for most victories by a pro—male or female—in her book, *Golf for Women*. "She won nine tournaments in one season. It proved to doubters that one player, if she was good

Nancy Lopez was golf's greatest young player. At age 15 she was already an established national star.

*Lopez attracted the
largest crowds of any
female golfer. In this
1978 photo, "Nancy's
Navy" (a take-off of
Palmer's "Arnie's
Army") follows her
around the course.*

enough, could dominate our tour. I still say that
today. If a player wants to, if she has that
desire, she can dominate."

Nancy's love affair with golf began when she
was in elementary school. Domingo Lopez
owned a small auto body shop in Roswell, New

Mexico. A good amateur player, he taught the game to his daughter rather than have her learn at a country club, partly because the family could not afford the lessons. Domingo had Nancy read dozens of instructional articles and books, but he also set aside $100 a month from the family earnings and spent it on Nancy's golf needs.

By the time she was 7, she was on the course nearly every day, practicing the strokes that would eventually lift her to greatness.

Nancy grew up playing on a typical municipal course in New Mexico. It was flat and dry and the greens were in so-so shape. "Learning to play in tough conditions like that really helped me develop as a golfer," she said. When you can play on courses where there are none of the advantages of a country club, you can handle anything in golf."

When she was 12, Nancy won the New Mexico amateur title. She won it two more times, then began competing—and winning—on the national level. By 1972, she'd twice won the U.S. Junior championship, the most important American tournament for teenagers.

"All I did as a kid was practice and play," she said. "I gave up boyfriends and I know I gave up part of growing up, where you can be carefree. My parents had sacrificed too much for me to put away the clubs and just play around.

"When I played badly, I would cry and my father would say, 'You can't see the ball if you cry.' And that made a lot of sense."

At Goddard High School, she played on the boys team, "which I really liked. It was a great challenge." In 1972, Goddard won the state championship with Nancy as one of the top players.

Nancy earned a golf scholarship to the University of Tulsa, where she played for two years. As a freshman, she entered the U.S.

Women's Open, against the best professionals in the world, and finished tied for third.

As a sophomore, she won the collegiate national crown and played in several international competitions. She made the All-America team and was the school's Female Athlete of the Year. But she also admitted she was not a good student. Her golf game had become so strong that she decided to turn pro in 1977. So all she did was finish second in her first three LPGA events and was rookie of the year.

But there would be tough times personally. Late in the 1977 season, Nancy's mother, Maria, died after undergoing surgery for appendicitis. Understandably, it took Nancy five months to get back her competitive drive. "That was very difficult; I missed my mom very much," Lopez said. "She understood what I was trying to do, but she would never know what I might accomplish."

Domingo took out a $50,000 loan from a bank to finance his daughter on the pro tour, but she won back that and much more within a year. In fact, she carried around her first check, for $800, for months, not wanting to cash it.

And, because of how well she responded to fans and how much the crowds loved her, she began making money in endorsements and for personal appearances, which made her far more comfortable as a pro than at first she thought she'd be.

"I was scared," she said of joining the tour. "I was afraid of being alone out there. I worried because I love to play, but I also wanted to have a family and not just play golf. Week after week of golf, moving from place to place, would make

In 1978, Lopez set a record by winning five straight tourneys. She won more money than any previous women's golfer.

it impossible to establish any kind of relationship. I had to ask myself, 'Was that going to happen to me?' 'Was I just going to play golf all my life?'"

She would play great golf, and eventually she would have an outstanding family life, too. By early 1978, Lopez—dedicating the season to her mother—was back on tour, but several players felt she was getting special treatment from the LPGA and from tournament organizers. Already hurting from her mother's death, now Nancy had to deal with being an outcast among some of the other women. "I began feeling and hearing the animosity growing," she said.

In her caddie, Roscoe Jones, she found a comforting sidekick. Jones would keep her focused on golf, try to keep her relaxed. Thanks to Jones, and Nancy's dad, and her boyfriend from Tulsa, Ronnie Benedettie, to whom she was engaged, Lopez was ready for big things. Bigger things than anyone had ever done in women's golf.

She won the Bent Tree Classic in Sarasota, Florida, her first pro victory. On the final hole, she had tears rolling down her cheeks as she walked to the green with the title secure. "I was thinking of my mom and how proud and excited she would have been," she said. "When I got on the green, she was all I could think about."

But the crowd was so adoring in its tribute to Nancy that she had no trouble finishing. And then, a pro champion for the first time, she broke down and cried. "I don't know what my mother's death did to me," she said, "except that somehow it made me more powerful."

It sure did. She won again in the next tournament, the Sunstar Classic in Los Angeles. And the fans were beginning to organize themselves, just as they did for Arnold Palmer on the men's tour. Arnie had his Army and Nancy now had her Navy.

She won again in May at Baltimore. Then she was first in New Jersey, and at the Golden Lights Championship, and heading into the LPGA Championship, one of the tour's four majors, Lopez was the hottest thing in sports. "I was on some ride," she said. "I felt I could birdie every hole, win every time I was on the course. I was so confident."

Her fellow golfers were in awe. "They've got the wrong person playing Wonder Woman on television," said Judy Rankin, one of the top players on tour.

"If she keeps this up," added Joanne Carner, one of Lopez's idols, "we might as well all just play for second place and give her the trophy."

The trophy for the LPGA Championship was one Nancy wanted very much. She began to feel the pressure of winning a major title and keeping the streak going. She had called off her wedding plans. "I'd really built up to that tournament," she recalled. "If I could just get onto the first tee and get going."

Lopez hit a monstrous drive on that first tee. That let out much of the tension. In the second round, Nancy was sensational. Later calling it the best round of her life, she had two eagles, four birdies, and no bogies. She was 8 under par for the round, and headed for a six-stroke victory and her first major title.

"Most golfers would have been drained by what Nancy was going through," Whitworth said. "But she wasn't through." The next week, Nancy won the Banker's Trust Tournament, giving her an LPGA record five straight wins. In half a year, she'd already won more than $150,000.

By the end of 1978, Nancy had won two more events, one in Europe, the other in Asia. She finished the year as the leading money winner and Player of the Year.

Many observers believed no player ever could match that feat. Nancy nearly did the next year, taking eight titles to sweep the awards once more. Included in her 1979 total were

repeat championships in the Sunstar, Coca-Cola, Golden Lights, and European events.

As great as her career was on the course, Nancy wasn't yet happy off it. She had a brief marriage to sportscaster Tim Melton. She began feeling uncomfortable with the constant attention away from golf, where she had little privacy.

Ray Volpe, the commissioner of the LPGA in the late 1970s, was heavy into marketing. He believed that building up Nancy as the savior of women's golf, the great superstar who would be

Lopez gives a birdie putt some encouragement as it heads for the cup on her way to winning the 1980 Sarah Coventry Tournament.

to the women's tour what Palmer was for the men, was the right approach.

It worked for a while, because the women needed someone the public could focus on. But it also created problems when tournament sponsors began thinking they must have Nancy Lopez make appearances for them and be in their event for it to be successful.

That was unfair to Nancy, who couldn't be everywhere all the time. And it was very unfair to the other excellent players on the LPGA tour. "There were times when I went back to the hotel and did nothing by cry," she said.

Her play didn't really suffer, though. Lopez no longer was winning eight or nine events a year, a pace that nobody could keep up. But she had only three victories in 1980 and in 1981, winning her second major, the Dinah Shore, in 1981. Then, in October 1982, she married Ray Knight, a baseball player who understood how tough the life of a pro athlete can be.

Together, Knight and Lopez built a strong marriage and a happy family. In 1983, Nancy gave birth to Ashley. Three years later, Nancy had another daughter, Erinn. In 1991, along came Torri.

Nancy cut back on her tour schedule as she and Ray—who became the manager of the Cincinnati Reds—raised their children. She still enjoys playing tour events, but not at the expense of time with the kids.

"During the school year, I come home from a tournament and sometimes I feel lost, like I don't know what's going on in their lives," she said. "I don't like that. Some people might think that trick-or-treating isn't a big deal. It's a big deal for me, because I've never gotten to do it much before. I enjoy the normal things: Going to lunch at school, substitute teaching for an hour. Those are the things that calm me and keep me from feeling guilty that I should be out practicing or playing."

Lopez entered the 1996 season with 47 career victories, including four majors. She qualified for the LPGA Hall of Fame in 1987 by winning at Sarasota, the site of her first tour championship. "My goal that first year was to win one tournament," Lopez said at the induction ceremonies. "I always set goals, and I never set this, making the Hall of Fame, as my goal. I said, 'Nobody could ever do that.'

"It's tough to get in. But it's fair—now that I'm in," she said jokingly. "That's a lot of tournaments with the competition the way it is.

"You think about the Hall of Fame and strive to get in when you first start playing on the tour, but you wonder if it will ever come," Lopez said. "It's very special getting into the Hall of Fame where there are so many great players. It's such an honor."

That's exactly what the other players in the Hall say about being in the company of Nancy Lopez, who has lived her dream.

4

BETSY KING

The favorite sport of Betsy King, a Hall of Fame golfer, is not golf. It's basketball. King even spent time as an assistant coach at Scottsdale (Arizona) Christian Academy during breaks from the women's golf tour. Maybe someday she and another hero of the Phoenix area, Charles Barkley, formerly of the NBA's Suns, can team up to coach or even buy a basketball team. For now, though, Betsy King remains one of the best golfers in the world.

At the end of 1993, King took the tour's final official event, the Toray Japan Queens Cup, for her 29th career win. As she had already won five majors—two U.S. Opens, two Dinah Shores and an LPGA crown—all she needed to make the LPGA Hall of Fame was one more tournament title.

Suddenly the woman who seemed to win everywhere she went had trouble coming up with another victory—even if it wasn't against

Betsy King waves to the gallery after a birdie during her win at the 1990 U.S. Women's Open.

top-flight talent. For a year and half she labored, often finishing a shot or two behind on the leaderboard. Then in 1995, she won the ShopRite Classic in New Jersey, and her entrance in the Hall was guaranteed.

"I felt like I played OK the last couple of years," King said. "I just think the level of competition has improved. It's harder to win. If you are off a little bit on your game, somebody else is going to be in there. I feel as competitive as ever, but it's a little easier to play now with that behind me."

It wasn't as if King never went through tough times as a professional golfer. And even when she was chasing the thirtieth win, it wasn't as if she was in a slump.

"It gets harder to win on tour all the time," King said. "There are so many good players out here and they all have the game to win in any week. You have to be tough physically and tough mentally. I was in position to win tournaments and just didn't do it during that span."

King did, however, collect more than $390,000 in her winless 1994 season—her first year without a title since 1984. She wound up in the top 10 an impressive 11 times and had two runner-up finishes.

In 1995, she was in the running in a few more events before she reached Somers Point, New Jersey, and the ShopRite Classic in late June.

The tournament was held about a two hours' drive from Reading, Pennsylvania, where Betsy grew up. Members of her family and dozens of friends came to the Greate Bay Resort and Country Club, hoping to see history.

Could King cooperate? After nearly 20 months, could she finally take that huge step into the most honored club in sports?

"We've always known how determined Betsy is," said her father, Dr. Weir King. "If there was any way for her to do something, she would find the way and do it."

It wasn't easy. She mishit her first shot of the day, sending it only 20 yards. "If you saw that tee shot on Number 1, you would never believe I'd be here," she said when the tournament ended. "I was kind of nervous and had a tough start."

Not one to ever give up, she made a 40-foot putt to par the hole. King birdied Numbers 4, 7, 8 to take the lead, but her bogey on Number 9 dropped her into a tie with Rosie Jones. Nine holes to go and Betsy knew she needed to relax. But she also knew what the fans and the television commentators were saying.

"It became a subject that was always mentioned," she said. "People mean well, but I'm so tired of being asked about it. I felt it was a little unfair that when I was close to the lead people would ask about the Hall."

The best way to cure that was to make the Hall of Fame. Betsy knew it, and she didn't back down from the challenge.

King sank a 14-foot birdie putt on Number 17 to break a tie and won it with a 12-footer for birdie on Number 18. After making her last putt, King threw her arms in the air and hugged her caddie, while the folks from Reading celebrated.

"The one word is just relief," said King, the 14th player in the LPGA Hall. "It was neat my parents were here and that so many people from Reading were here. It's exciting, but I was just happy that I don't have to deal with it anymore.

"I'm very proud to be a member of the Hall of Fame. But accomplishments like this mean nothing if I didn't have family and friends to share them with."

In her acceptance speech, King thanked what she called her many families—most importantly, her parents, Weir and Helen King, and her brother, Lee.

King joined the LPGA tour in 1977 after winning a college championship at Furman University. It took her seven years to win her first pro championship, and she just kept right on going.

She was LPGA Player of the Year in 1984, 1989, and 1993. From 1984-1989, she won 20 tournaments, more than any golfer on any tour. She was the first woman to win $500,000 in a single LPGA season, then the first to go over $600,000. Betsy also was the first to pass $5 million in career earnings. And she had her own tournament, the Betsy King LPGA Classic, added to the 1996 tour.

For all of those achievements, King might be best remembered for her charity work. A member of the LPGA Christian Fellowship, she organized Habitat for Humanity house-buildings in Arizona, North Carolina, and Tennessee.

Following the 1993 and 1994 seasons, King and a group of LPGA players traveled to Romania, a nation torn by civil war earlier in the decade. Romanians, especially youngsters, had a difficult time finding food, clothing, and housing. "Just 48 hours after winning a tournament and clinching player of the year, I'm in the streets of Bucharest seeing kids almost starving to death, people struggling to get by," she said. "It opened my eyes."

King handed out food and candy and helped pay for installation of plumbing and indoor heating for one family. "We were standing in snow, freezing, dealing with young children who live under a train station," she said. "Seeing it changed my life. We experienced first-hand what it is like to live without the basics that we take for granted."

The deeply religious King sang with a church group of teenagers at a train station, which she called more touching than anything she ever felt on any golf course or basketball court.

"Hearing 'Amazing Grace' so far from home and in those circumstances was very moving,"said Betsy King, who has proved to be a star on more than just the golf course.

5

PAT BRADLEY

In 1986, Pat Bradley had perhaps the best season any women's golfer has managed. She won six times, including three major tournaments. She won the Player of the Year award. She won the Vare Trophy for the lowest scoring average on the LPGA tour, an honor every player strives for.

In 1987, Pat Bradley won just one tournament. Her earnings dropped from an incredible (for then) $492,021 to $140,132.

In 1988, Pat Bradley was almost a forgotten name in the sport.

"After such big seasons in 1986 and 1987, something went wrong with me," she said. "I couldn't sleep. I was tired. Something was physically wrong with me, but I was in denial and I wouldn't admit it. I'd won almost $500,000 in '86 and $150,000 in '87. Suddenly, I plummeted to $15,000 in '88. Finally, I realized I had to do something about it."

Pat Bradley coaxing a putt in 1984, before she was diagnosed with Graves' Disease.

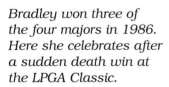
*Bradley won three of
the four majors in 1986.
Here she celebrates after
a sudden death win at
the LPGA Classic.*

For more than two years, Bradley suffered severe headaches and fatigue. Her heart raced at 150 beats a minute when she was sitting down. Her body shook and trembled. She had Graves' Disease, which is an overactive thyroid. Another great golfer, Ben Crenshaw, suffered from the same disease.

"It felt like my body was racing 100 mph 24 hours a day," Bradley said. "I had no idea what was going on. I had tremendous palpitations of my heart. I thought my heart was coming through my chest. I thought I had created these symptoms in my mind."

Pat thought she could handle the situation herself, because she believed they were emotional problems.

"I had never been sick in my life, so I didn't think there was anything physically wrong with me," she said. "I thought I was creating the symptoms in my own mind, trying to maintain the high level of performance I had set for myself in 1986. I was not that ready to run to a psychiatrist and say, 'OK, put me in the suit and take me away.' "

With the help of radioactive treatments and medication, Pat was able to control the illness by December.

By April 1989, one year after learning she had the disease, Bradley was a force on the tour again. She won the All Star-Centinela Hospital Classic, ending a two-year drought. She earned more than $400,000. Most noteworthy of all, she had returned to the level of golfing legend.

6

PATTY SHEEHAN

Patty Sheehan was sitting at Candlestick Park, ready to enjoy the third game of the World Series between the San Francisco Giants and Oakland A's. Then her world began to shake, along with the lives of millions of others in the Bay Area.

The 1989 earthquake had a big effect on Sheehan. She survived just fine—a bit rattled perhaps, but healthy. Her house in Scotts Valley, Calif., a 4,000 square-foot showplace, was demolished. And she had no insurance to cover it. Lost in the quake was much of Patty's collection of 35 trophies from her Hall of Fame golfing career. Many of those trophies were irreplaceable.

"As I drove up the road, I looked at my vegetable garden. There were two wooden cows

Patty Sheehan watches her long birdie putt sink at the LPGA World Championship in 1986—the same year she won the LPGA Samaritan Award.

still standing up in the garden. It was like a victory," Sheehan said. "Then when I opened the front door of the house, there were about four-inch gaps between the front door and the rest of the house. It was a mess. It was as if somebody had gone into the house and ransacked it like they do in the movies. Only this was real life."

The worst part of the reality was that Patty would need all of her winnings from an already-superb golf career, plus whatever she could win in the next year or more, to recover from the lack of insurance. "I thought I did have insurance," she explained. "To find out I didn't have any was unsettling, to say the least. Most people in the area didn't have the insurance, because it was too expensive."

Most people aren't like Sheehan, however. Few have her determination, and she proved it in the first event of the 1990 season, winning the Jamaica Open. The money would come in handy, but what meant even more to Patty was the way she dealt with her problems. She had to overcome them, so she did—quickly and convincingly. "It was tough," Sheehan said. "The good thing is that I learned a lot about myself, my family, friends and neighbors. I think through it all that the basic thing I learned was about putting my priorities in the wrong place. As quick as it took to destroy bridges, houses and people's lives, it put mine back together. It made me grow up and mature."

Since then, Sheehan has become one of the biggest winners in women's golf. She has been as good as just about anyone in the 1990s, winning five times in 1990, once in 1991, three times the next year and in 1994, and twice in 1995.

Four of her six major championships have come in this decade, including the U.S.

Sheehan kisses the trophy for winning the $450,000 Japan Women's Classic in 1988. She won that year's earning title on the U.S. tour.

Women's Open in 1993 and 1994. Also in 1993, when she won the Standard Register PING tournament in Phoenix, Patty qualified for the LPGA Hall of Fame.

"The closer I got to the Hall of Fame, the more I thought about, and the more I didn't want to think about it," Sheehan said after making a birdie on the last hole of the Phoenix event to punctuate her five-shot win. "It's one of those catch-22s where you try to stay away from jinxing yourself, kind of tiptoe around the issue. But as I got closer, I thought about it a lot more."

She also thought about Pat Bradley, another golfing legend who stopped winning for nearly four years after getting her 30th crown and entry into the Hall. "Look at the problems Pat was having," Sheehan said. "She won 30 and hasn't really done much since. I think she lost her motivation. I didn't want that to happen to me. I didn't want to become complacent, I don't want to roll over and die. I don't want to stop and I don't want to stop trying."

Considered one of the most determined athletes in America, Sheehan is known for handling bad times and turning them into good. Perhaps the greatest proof of that came in 1990, when Sheehan blew an eight-shot lead at the U.S. Women's Open and lost to Betsy King.

It was one of the biggest collapses in golf history and certainly could have ruined a weaker person. "I won't be able to forget this," Sheehan said after losing an 8-shot lead over the last 23 holes of a 36-hole windup caused by bad weather; usually golfers play 18 holes a day. "Hopefully, I'll learn from it. It's not the end of the world."

She made sure it wasn't by turning it into her most successful season, earning $732,618 and winning five times. Just one week after her failure at the Open, she came right back to finish second at Youngstown, Ohio, losing a playoff to Beth Daniel. "Coming back after last week, it was really tough to even tee it up," she said. "In that respect, I played very well. I played well all week after last week's disappointment."

From there, she has won at least one tournament every year and four more majors, including the U.S. Women's Open twice.

Patty also is a champion away from the course. She sponsored a home for troubled teenage girls, runs tournaments for various charities back home in Reno, Nevada, and helps fund golf programs for youths. She is active in the Special Olympics and aided a group that assists women being treated for drug and alcohol abuse.

In 1986, Patty received the LPGA Samaritan Award, mainly for her work with Tigh Sheehan, the home in California she helped establish for teenage girls. "I originally got involved by giving clothes, then it got to a point where I bought a pool table," Patty recalled. "It just kept snowballing and I just kept doing more and more."

Among her activities were buying a house, getting another tour golfer, Lauren Howe, involved, and purchasing another house. At one point, Sheehan was involved with four houses in Soquel, California. "The girls are not very impressed with my achievements," she said when she won the 1986 award. "They think more about boys and dancing than what I'm doing. When I go to visit, I try to keep it light and happy and a little upbeat. The kids don't talk about their situations much, because they talk about it all the time with counselors. I may kid them about dinner or about their boyfriends. We play music and dance. We really have a good time with each other."

Patty, who joined the LPGA tour in 1980 and won a tournament within a year, more recently was honored by the Women's Sports Foundation. She won the Flo Hyman Award, which is named for an Olympic volleyball player who died of a rare disease. Sheehan joined tennis greats Chris Evert and Martina Navratilova; another golfing legend, Nancy Lopez; and Olympic track champions Jackie Joyner-Kersee and Evelyn Ashford as winners of the award. "Flo Hyman was an inspiration to all athletes in the world," Patty said, "and to be selected for this honor is kind of mind-boggling. This means a lot to me, because I'm being recognized not only for what I have done on the course, but for life outside my sporting arena, as well."

She has been a champion in both places.

7

THE NEW WAVE

Many of the top stars in women's golf in the last 20 years haven't quite made it to the level of the greats such as Nancy Lopez, Joanne Carner, Betsy King, Pat Bradley, and Patty Sheehan. Still, they deserve recognition and applause for excellent careers. Judy Rankin, Beth Daniel, Amy Alcott, Donna Caponi, Ayoko Okamoto, Hollis Stacy, Dottie Pepper, Meg Mallon, and Annika Sorenstam have, in various spans, been the best players on tour.

Daniel and Alcott both stood close to qualifying for the LPGA Hall of Fame as they entered the 1996 season. Their ability to remain at the top level for so long is a tribute to their skills and determination.

Nowadays, the strength of the Swedish golf program has been exceptional. Sorenstam led

Beth Daniel teeing off, en route to her victory at the 1990 LPGA Championship.

the LPGA in earnings in 1995. Countrywomen Liselotte Neumann, Helen Alfredsson, and Carin Hj Koch lead the wave of Swedish stars. Neumann was the first Swede to make a breakthrough in America, winning the 1988 U.S. Women's Open and being named LPGA Rookie of the Year. Four years later, Alfredsson was Rookie of the Year. In 1994, Sorenstam won that award and was the 1995 U.S. Open champion.

"Golf is now a game of the people in Sweden," said Koch. "It's not as expensive as it is in America. There are lots more good players in Sweden and they will be coming here soon."

Sorenstam credits players such as Okamoto of Japan and Neumann with blazing a trail for the current wave of non-American stars. "I think more foreign players are getting aware that other foreign players are playing," Sorenstam said. "If one or two players open it up by playing well, you understand, 'Well, maybe I can do it.' "

Another top foreigner is Laura Davies, the longest hitter in the women's game. Off the tee, she can hit the ball 300 yards, which is longer than some of the male pros. She averaged 265 yards on her drives in 1995.

Davies, a native of England, even played in a four-person exhibition in Australia against three men early in 1996. A winner of 15 tournaments worldwide in a two-year span, she regularly outdrove Tom Watson, one of the all-time greats in men's golf.

She won $9,750 in the "Skins Game," in which players compete for money on each hole. "It was great fun," she said, "but I am not looking to join the men very often. This was just a fun thing to do."

There are so many good players on the LPGA Tour today that the 58th leading money winner in 1995 earned more than $100,000.

"Something to remember about the tour is that there are more women than you can imagine who can play well in a week and win the

Annika Sorenstam, seen here lining up a tricky putt, is one of the bright new stars on the LPGA circuit.

tournament," King said. "For anyone to win once or twice a year is a good year."

Some of the names to remember, players with the talent and drive to become stars, perhaps Hall of Famers, are Michelle McGann, Kelly Robbins, Karrie Webb, Lora Fairclough, Brandie Burton, Donna Andrews, Alison Nicholas, and Wendy Ward.

"It takes more than just having the game," Carner said. "You need to have the makeup to handle the pressure and to forget when things go wrong, not carry over your mistakes to the next shot and the next one.

"Nearly all of the women out on the tour now have the shots. They play and learn when they are kids and then through the college programs, and they become excellent shotmakers. What you wonder about is if they have the toughness and the patience and the desire to be the best. If they do, then they're headed toward the top."

One player who seemed ready to reach the top was Jan Stephenson of Australia. At first, Stephenson became popular with television, newspapers, and magazines because of her striking looks. But that, of course, is not what women's golf is about; do you hear commentators mention how handsome a men's player is when he's running off birdie after birdie?

Stephenson has won her share of tournaments—16 since joining the LPGA tour in 1974, including the 1982 LPGA Championship and the U.S. Women's Open in 1983. But she's never become a dominant player because of a string of bad luck usually resulting in injuries. In 1981, she broke a foot, and in 1987, she sustained four broken ribs in an auto accident. That year, however, was one of her best on tour, with three victories. Unfortunately, the 1987 Konica San Jose Classic was her last win.

Three years later, Stephenson was attacked by a thief in a Miami parking lot. Her ring finger was badly broken, and she never has been the same golfer since the incident. "The doctors all said this would be a nice way to gracefully bow out, because we feel your career may be over," Stephenson said. "I refused to admit that."

She underwent three hours a day of therapy on the finger, but Stephenson could not recapture the strength of her game, her ability to hit long iron shots. "I had no idea at the time it was going to be as major as it was," she said. After her attacker was caught, "I told the judge I just wanted his finger broken. I didn't want him to go to jail. I just wanted him to go through what I have gone through."

Sadly, Stephenson has not gone through any winning times this decade. Several other players believe in her, but does Jan have that belief?

"When you've been away from it and haven't really been under the gun, I think the hardest thing to get back is being able to trust yourself," Bradley said. "Deep down inside you know it's there, it's just allowing yourself to trust it."

The legends of women's golf always have had that trust. It was what made the pioneers believe they could make a professional tour work in the first place. It was what the next great wave used to carry the sport to a higher level. And it is what the stars of today—and tomorrow—will use to create more queens of the links.

STATISTICS

Player	Born	JT	CV	MV	CE	HF	Died
Pat Bradley	Mar. 24, 1951	1974	31	6	$5, 141,019	1992	
Betsy King	Aug. 13, 1955	1977	30	5	$5,374,022	1995	
Nancy Lopez	Jan. 6, 1957	1977	47	3	$4,275,685	1987	
Patty Sheehan	Oct. 27, 1956	1980	34	6	$4,788,546	1993	
Babe Zaharias	June 26,1914	1951	31	5	$66,237	1951	9/27/1

JT	Joined LPGA Tour
CV	Career Pro Victories
MV	Major Pro Victories
CE	Career Earnings
HF	Inducted Into Hall of Fame

Suggestions For Further Reading

Alcott, Amy, with Don Wade. *Amy Alcott's Guide to Women's Golf.* New York: Dutton, 1991.

Glenn, Rhonda. *Illustrated History of Women's Golf.* Dallas: Taylor Publications, 1991.

Mann, Carol. *The 19th Hole.* Stamford, CT: Longmeadow Press, 1993.

Sheehan, Patty, with Betty Hicks. *Patty Sheehan on Golf.* Dallas: Taylor Publications, 1996.

About the Author

BARRY WILNER has been a sportswriter for the *Associated Press* for 20 years. In that time, he has covered, the Super Bowl, Olympics, World Cup, Stanley Cup finals, and many other sporting events. He has written books on hockey, soccer, swimming, and Olympic sports. He is the author of *Dan Marino* in Chelsea's "Football Legends" series, and Reggie Miller in the "Basketball Legends" series. He lives in Garnerville, NY, with his wife, Helene, daughters Nicole, Jamie, and Tricia, and son Evan.

INDEX

PICTURE CREDITS

AP/Wide World: 2, 6, 9, 10, 13, 18, 21, 25, 28, 31, 34, 37, 40, 46, 48, 50, 59; Archive Photos: 22, 53, 56.